RTÉ

FAIR·CITY

BY

BRIAN GALLAGHER

ROONEY
MEDIA
GRAPHICS

Acknowledgements

Writing a book about a long-running TV series involves a lot of research, and I've been fortunate to encounter a great deal of goodwill while gathering my material.

My sincere thanks go to Niall Mathews and Sinead O'Connor who first said yes to the project, and to all the staff working on the show who so patiently bore the presence of a lurking writer asking endless questions. My particular thanks go to former Series Producer Eleanor Cunny, who helped in so many ways, and to Kevin McHugh, John Lynch, Elaine Walsh, Tara O'Brien, Marie-Claire Cassidy, David O'Sullivan, Niki Brately, Mary Martin, Paul Fitzgerald, Mary Morrow, Alan Archbold, Eddie Finlay, Sean O'Briain, Michael Sweeney, Mary Boyd, Clare Beegan, Karen Nolan, Joe Canavan, Ian Pike, Hilary Reynolds, Claire O'Sullivan, Liz Nugent, Sharon McGlone and Ann Myler for their co-operation and support.

In the RTÉ library I'd like to thank Margaret Hogan, Emma Keogh, Pearl Quinn, Tom Holton, Tina Byrne and Amy Kerr for all their assistance, and at the *RTÉ Guide* a special thanks goes to John Cooney and David Mahon.

Among the cast I'm grateful for the time afforded to me, by Una Crawford O'Brien, Pat Nolan, Sarah McDowall, Tony Tormey, Jean Costello and Tom Jordan.

Denise Dunne, the maker of the documentary *Fair City – the Ten Commandments*, generously gave me access to research that she had done, and likewise Tara O'Brien, the show's publicist, helped me to unearth material I would never have found otherwise.

I'm grateful to Evelyn Pender and Keith Adams for reading the manuscript in draft form and for sharing their thoughts with me, and at Rooney Media Graphics I'd like to thank Pat Rooney, Niall Reilly and Dan Moody for making it a pleasure to work on this project.

Finally a word of thanks to Pat Moylan, Claudia Carroll and Clare Dowling for their encouragement and support, and to my family, Miriam, Orla and Peter, who, as ever, make it all possible.

The Doyle Family

BALLIE NA CARRAIG
CARRIGSTOWN   9

TO KATHLEEN KELLY
IN THANKS FOR ALL THE SUPPORT

Foreword By Gerry Ryan

There's no doubt about it, we've come a long way. Time was when someone going on the pill in an Irish TV series could cause a rumpus – yes, folks, it actually happened with *The Riordans*, and it created a fuss even though the fictitious character involved was a married woman.

Fast forward a decade and a half, and we have Fair City being launched into a decidedly less innocent world. Nevertheless Fair City has still caused blood pressure to rise on occasions, and over the years it hasn't shied away from tackling thorny subjects. Mostly though it's been fun to watch, and in the way of TV soaps, it's sucked lots of us into the colourful world of Carrigstown.

We've booed villains like Billy Meehan, watched fascinated to see if Malachy would leave the priesthood for Kay, reeled in disbelief at Christy's taste in sweaters and despaired of Barry ever finding a woman who wouldn't break his heart.

And now with INSIDE FAIR CITY the archives have been trawled to give us a highly entertaining record of the show. So whether you're an avid fan, a closet viewer, or even someone who says "I don't really watch it, but sometimes I see it when it's on at home" (often the most well-informed of viewers), here's a chance both to travel down memory lane and to have a peek behind the scenes at Ireland's favourite soap. Happy reading…

Gerry Ryan

Contents

Photo Credits
Photographs © RTÉ Stills Library. Additional material by Rooney Media Graphics. Cover photograph of Stella Fehilly and Jamie Belton courtesy TV Now magazine, cover photograph of Orlaith Rafter courtesy Mike Concannon, cover photograph of George McMahon courtesy of Kyran O'Brien, Adare Productions.

Contents

It was 1989, the year

Charlie Haughey was still Taoiseach, Jack

the Berlin Wall fell.

Charlton was manager of the Irish soccer squad and Mick MacCarthy was his team captain. People were dancing to Swing the Mood by Jive Bunny and the Mastermixers. In the autumn Cork won the All Ireland Final in football, and Tipperary won it in hurling. And on September the 18th a new drama series began on RTÉ. Fair City was born.

In its first year Fair City

went out just once a week, and when the season ended there was a five month break before the next episode went on air the following September – a far cry from the present situation of broadcasting four times a week, fifty-two weeks a year.

Much has changed in Ireland over those eventful sixteen years and Fair City too has adapted. While still setting out primarily to entertain, the programme has nevertheless reflected the changes taking place in Irish society and has frequently gripped, and sometimes even shocked its viewers as it dramatised the lives of the residents of Carrigstown.

But how does an idea go from being a notion in a writer's head to appearing on-screen – and to being seen by over half a million viewers?

It's an interesting journey, so let's make it together, and see what happens inside Fair City.

Early Days

Margaret Gleeson, who previously worked on *Tolka Row* and *The Riordans,* was the show's first Executive Producer.

In 1988 RTÉ decided to produce an urban drama series based in Dublin, and a transmission date of September 1989 was decided upon, which gave about a year to create the series from scratch.

With a team that included producers Paul Cusack and David McKenna, and Script Editor Tony Holland, Margaret Gleeson began putting in place the many components needed for a drama series.

Linda and Jack

Barron Place, a narrow cul-de-sac in Drumcondra, was chosen as the street on which many of the characters would live, in a fictional district called Carrigstown.

As work progressed and actors and writers were hired, the show operated under the working title of *Northsiders*. The initial commitment from RTÉ was for a series of thirteen episodes, and it was agreed that the show would open with an hour-long pilot episode.

There was a pioneering spirit abroad in those early days – houses in Barron Place were used for dressing rooms, and for serving tea and coffee – and everyone on the show worked hard to meet the transmission deadline.

Jimmy

Paul

Barry

Early Days

Finally the show was ready to air, with the first episode, written by Peter Sheridan, being broadcast on Tuesday September 18th 1989.

Lili

Paddy　　　　　　　　　　　　*Mary*

In its first season Fair City had a cast of twenty-two, and had eight writers – today it has a cast of over forty, and has thirty writers.

Early Days

The opening episode attracted a massive audience of 1.06 million viewers. It was directed by Chris Clough, who went on to produce *Ballykissangel*.

Anne

Johnny

WHAT THE PRESS SAID

"The characters seemed real enough, the setting was brilliantly realized, the acting was first-class, much better than anything in imported soaps, and the plot was engagingly plausible."
EAMON DUNPHY
Sunday Independent

"It's funny, it has real people and it looks very good indeed. It's 'Fair City' and it looks like Monday nights on RTE 1 will never be quite the same again."
BRENDAN GLACKEN
Irish Times

"RTE's new urban soap looks like being a winner."
EDDIE HOLT
Irish Independent

Dolores

Hannah

Hughie, Natalie and Baby Kevin

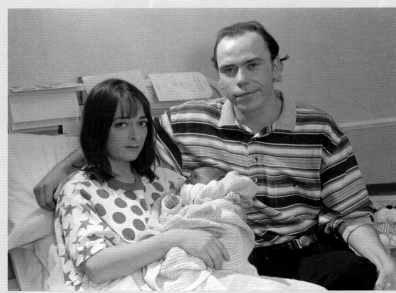

Clancey and Anne

Charlie and Mags

Bela

Kay

There have been big changes

since the pioneering days shown in the previous pages, and to facilitate producing today's quota of over two hundred episodes a year the show has to be planned and produced with military-like precision. So let's look at some of the key elements in keeping Carrigstown ticking over.

Harry

Early Days

The Executive Producer

Niall Mathews - Executive Producer
Fair City

The executive producer of Fair City is like the managing director of a medium sized company. At any given time there will be approximately one hundred people working on the show, comprising office staff, studio personnel, writers and cast.

The responsibility for the smooth operation of these various functions lies with the executive producer, Niall Mathews. His role involves allocating the budget, casting, approving story development and scripting, appointing directors and overseeing the many technical aspects involved in producing a show four nights a week, fifty-two weeks a year.

The executive producer is assisted by a series producer, Frank Hand, who is responsible for all aspects of the day to day running of the show, and by three assistant producers, Michael Sweeney, Sean O'Briain and Mary Martin who have responsibility for casting, locations and scripting.

Niall Mathews was appointed as executive producer on Fair City in 1990, and since then – apart from the period between 1994 and 1998, when Declan Eames and John Lynch respectively were in charge – he has been at the helm of what has turned out to be one of RTÉ's most popular programmes.

Niall believes that part of reason for the show's success is the flexible way in which the series is structured. Unlike Glenroe, for example, Fair City has never been reliant on a central family, but rather has various groupings of characters, any of which can be brought to the fore when carrying a major story. In this way the series doesn't suffer if a family or a group of characters hasn't got a naturally-occurring story at a particular time – the focus can simply be turned onto whatever group has got a story that's worth telling.

As executive producer, Niall Mathews sets a lot of store on making sure that stories for the series will engage viewers emotionally. An example he quotes is how a story about a character having an illness mustn't simply be a series of medical events, but, as in the case of Nicola having breast cancer, there must also be drama and human interest – as happened when Nicola lost her partner to her sister, while simultaneously having to cope with her illness.

Memorable storylines for Niall would include:

Kay, Malachy and the abortion.

The Sorcha and Ross relationship and
the fall-out from it.

The pirate radio story.

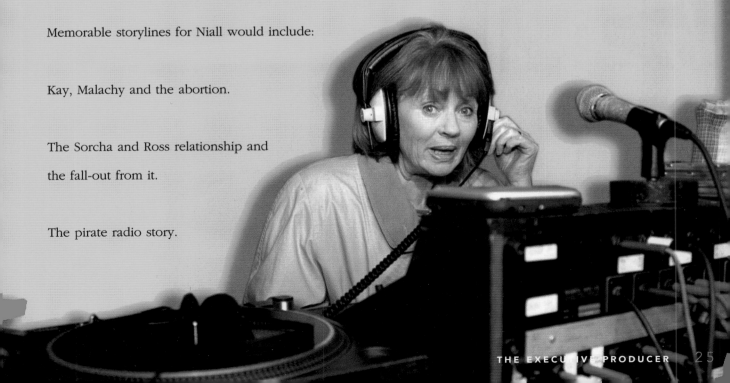

The Series Editor

The Series Editor, Kevin McHugh

Kevin McHugh began as script editor on Fair City in 1994 and by now has edited over one thousand episodes. When he started there were 64 episodes a year; last season there were 208.

Kevin's background as a theatre director gave him a lot of experience in working with new writers – "making the story live" is how he describes his role. Most stories are conceived by a dedicated story team, although at times actors and other writers come up with stories – sometimes they are accepted, sometimes not.

"An idea is not a story," is one of Kevin McHugh's dictums. Nor is an anecdote enough, there must be potential for a story to develop. A plotline must engage the character involved. As Kevin says "It's not a story *about* Charlie, it's *Charlie's story.*" And occasionally a

potentially great story won't work because it would clash with elements of a character's personality as already established onscreen.

On Fair City no subject is regarded as taboo, but when handling contentious stories consideration has to be given to both the broadcast time and the general sensibility of the show's audience.

Story is the key to everything else. It allows the characters - the central feature of the show – to take on a life.

Memorable storylines for Kevin would include:

Barry's breakdown.

Dolores, Harry and the death of Jessica.

Malachy leaving the priesthood to be with Kay.

How the story

At the start of the year the series editor and the senior storyline writer discuss the story outlines for that year.

For example, in the story that began with Barry's relationship with Sorcha, it was decided to show how the break-up would affect Barry's life. The arc of the story over the following twelve months showed Barry losing his job, losing his self-respect, taking the giant step of admitting the need for psychiatric help, and the slow process of his recovery.

FROM PAGE TO STAGE

comes to be told

Story Meeting

Having decided

with the series editor what the principal stories will be for the season, the senior storyline writer then takes these ideas to the story team. At any given time there will usually be four writers on this team and their job is to generate and develop story.

These stories will then be proposed to the executive producer and the series editor.

A further meeting will then take place with scripting and research staff, and after much discussion the main thrust of the stories will be established. A document fleshing out these stories will be sent to all the scriptwriters.

Stage

With the principal elements of the stories decided, the scripting department now has to tackle the complicated job of working out where and when the stories can be played out. This is determined by how many scenes can be shot in a day, what sets are at their disposal, actor availability, and even considerations such as sunrise and sunset – which determine whether an outdoor scene can be filmed in daylight or whether it will be shot as a night

scene. Location sequences that can't be filmed on the RTÉ lot will also be decided at this stage.

A document called a first draft breakdown is now sent to each script writer and this breaks down each particular episode into a suggested sequence of scenes and locations. The scriptwriters then meet everyone else on the script team and each scriptwriter makes specific suggestions regarding his or her particular episode. When these have been teased out a revised breakdown document is sent to each scriptwriter containing these changes and confirming the altered breakdown of scenes and locations.

At this stage the scriptwriters go to work, with a deadline of approximately two weeks to have each episode finished. Fair City works on a three week cycle, with four episodes per week, so twelve scriptwriters will normally take on each batch of episodes, which will be written three to four months before their transmission dates.

When these episodes are written they are submitted to the series editor, Kevin McHugh, who is in charge

of all script editing. Notes will be given to each writer as the editor strives to eliminate repetition, sharpen scenes generally and ensure a smooth transition in story terms from one episode to the next. Occasionally there will be a need for considerable re-writes, but the second draft that the scriptwriters now undertake will mostly involve fine-tuning and nips and tucks.

Stage

The second draft is written in a matter of days and then submitted to the series editor. Once the editor is satisfied with this draft the script will be printed and distributed to the production staff. A meeting will be held and the practicalities of the script will be studied, to ensure that everything described by the writer can actually be filmed. The script will then go back to the series editor who will ensure that any changes that have been made don't damage the unfolding of the storyline.

Then, finally, the script is given to whichever director has been allocated the episode involved, and later still to the actors cast in the episode.

>LENNY
I think this is probably as good a spot as any.

>ROBIN
For what?

>LENNY
For giving you this.

>
LENNY TAKES A JEWELLER'S CASE FROM HIS POCKET AND GIVES IT TO ROBIN.
SHE OPENS IT AND WE SEE AN IMPRESSIVE ENGAGEMENT RING. ROBIN IS
GOBSMACKED. LENNY TAKES HER HAND.

>LENNY
Robin...will you marry me?

>
ROBIN IS OVERCOME. SURPRISED, THRILLED,
ALMOST SPEECHLESS.

>ROBIN
God. Lenny...

>
ROBIN WRAPS HER ARMS AROUND HIM.

>LENNY
Is that a yes?

>
ROBIN LOOKS AT HIM AND SMILES WARMLY.

>ROBIN
Yes, Lenny. Oh yes...

>
ROBIN KISSES HIM.

<u>**END OF EPISODE.**</u>

Scriptwriters

Presently there are thirty scriptwriters.

All of them have come through an involved selection process that begins with a meeting with the series editor. A writer may then be asked to write sample scenes. If the sample scenes impress the series editor sufficiently the writer may be commissioned to write a shadow script. This is a full script, exactly as would be done for an actual episode, but one that will never be broadcast. If the shadow script is also deemed to be of the required calibre, the writer will usually then be commissioned to write an episode for broadcasting.

In general it is assumed that any established Fair City writer will be capable of writing any episode. Occasionally however, the series editor will allocate an episode to a specific writer, on the grounds of a particular skill or area of knowledge that the writer has that applies to that episode.

Love is good,

Love is good – but URST is better . . .

URST? No, not the capital of some former Soviet Republic, but a vital factor in driving the storyline of a soap, URST stands for **unresolved sexual tension.**

In real life most people want love, happiness, contentment – the very things that are the kiss of death for drama. Which is why soaps thrive on unrequited love, illicit affairs, ill-suited couples and betrayal. So although viewers may enjoy a fairy-tale romance occasionally, for every love story that works out, there are lots of couples that never make it . . .

Matches **NOT** made in Heaven

Research

David O'Sullivan

Do nurses in intensive care units wear scrubs? Does a barrister address a judge as Your Honour or My Lord? Questions like these and a thousand and one other queries routinely land on the desk of David O'Sullivan, the Series Story Associate.

A great deal of effort goes into researching the technical detail needed to make a story seem credible on screen. As researcher for the series, David O'Sullivan is involved at every stage of a story's development, initially liaising with the senior story-line writer, and later providing whatever information is needed by the script editor, the executive producer, the individual scriptwriters, the directors, and the actors.

Over the years a file has been built up in the Fair City office of experts in legal, medical and other professional fields whose advice can be sought when needed. If a particular story calls for detailed technical knowledge then not only will the story team and the writers be given the necessary information, but completed scripts will be studied by an expert in the field involved, to make certain that nothing shown on screen is inaccurate.

A balance has to be struck between the need for accuracy and the need of a television series to dramatise its characters' lives. David O'Sullivan quotes Alfred Hitchcock's theory that "drama is real life with the boring bits removed." So yes, Fair City will seek to make its characters' dilemmas interesting and dramatic, but always with an eye on accuracy and the need for credibility.

In stories such as Robin's bulimia, Nicola's breast cancer and Barry's psychiatric problems it was important not just to be technically accurate but also to handle the stories sensitively. This can only be done with detailed knowledge to hand, and so actors who are called on to carry a specialised storyline usually work in tandem with the researcher, often in addition to doing research of their own.

Right up to the last minute the story associate can still receive queries – sometimes having to answer unforeseen questions that arise as late as the day of shooting. And until an episode is finally "in the can", the researcher is responsible for the accuracy of everything that appears on screen.

Fair City Trivia

- Ignatius Joseph Mary was the name originally bestowed upon - Bela!

- When Eunice sold her house to the Doyles she uprooted plants from the garden and took the plants with her – along with the seat from the toilet - on the day of the move.

- Kay's first love was Danny McCusker, who came into Kay's life again after many years, only to be shot in a gangland killing.

- Years before Roddy Doyle used the name in a Booker Prize-winning novel, Paddy Clarke was one of the original characters in Fair City.

- Farrah, the daughter of Christy and Renee, has been played by three different actresses.

- A cult called The Church of the Children of Eternal Light had two members in Carrigstown - Noeleen and Stephen.

- Rita met her future husband, Bela, at the Matchmaking Festival in Lisdoonvarna.

- When it comes to being unlucky in love, it's hard to beat Barry. Three of his relationships have ended with his partners being unfaithful; Linda with Bela, Niamh with Paul, and Sorcha with Ross.

- Lorcan has had three fathers; a natural father he's never met, an adoptive father, Malachy, and a step-father, Billy Meehan - whom he killed!

- Fourteen years after the violent death of his son, Tony, Charlie accidentally killed Pat's son, Johnno.

- Dolores and Harry's baby daughter, Jessica, was played on-screen by a baby boy.

- Carol seems to have a particular attraction for the Meehan family. Both Billy and his sister Chrisso each wanted to have a relationship with her.

- Due to a misunderstanding when he was in Africa on UN duty, Paschal lost his true love, Lily, and didn't see her again until forty-two years later, when they met in Carrigstown.

IT WAS THE NINETEEN NINETIES AND IRELAND WAS READY FOR ANOTHER TABOO TO BE BROKEN . . .

FAIR CITY'S FIRST GAY KISS

Directors

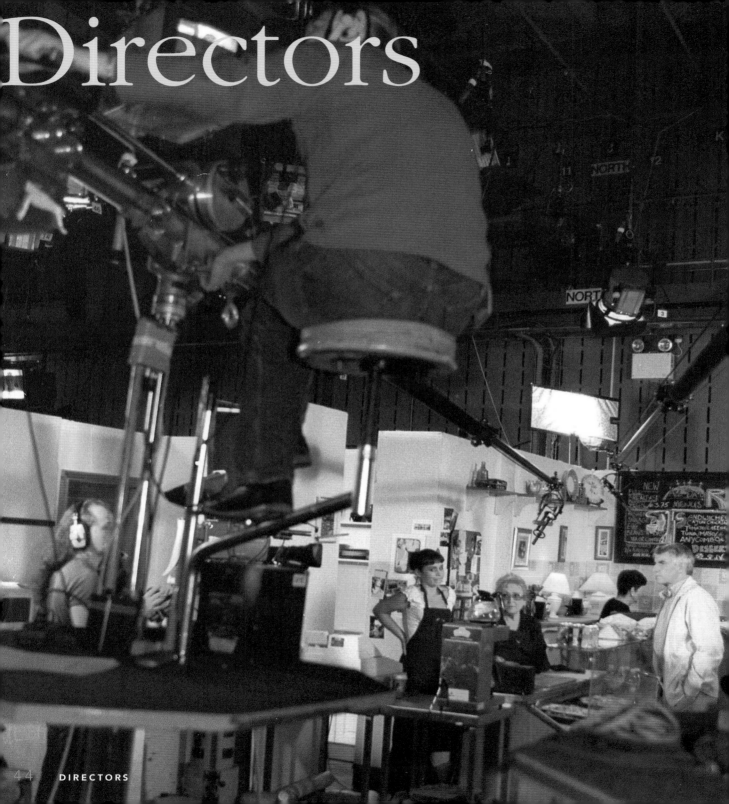

Directors

The job of the director is a wide-ranging one, requiring diverse skills such as rehearsing the actors, organising shooting, overseeing editing, and deciding on the amount of dubbing required. Most Fair City directors are RTÉ staff members, but outside directors are also brought in on contract, as required.

Staff directors working on the show direct as many as thirty to forty episodes a year. With four episodes being filmed every week, each director works on a five-week cycle.

WEEK 1

This week is taken up with scripting. The director will study every scene to be filmed and will decide where actors will stand, at what point in a scene they'll sit, where they'll walk, etc. The director will also decide on all camera angles and shot sizes for the four episodes involved.

WEEK 2

This is the week of shooting. Saturday is dedicated to rehearsing, and the director will discuss their performances with the actors as much as possible at this stage, as there will be little time for detailed guidance during the rigorous shooting schedules that will apply for the rest of the week.

On Monday the director will attend a producer's run, which is akin to a dress rehearsal of all four episodes. From Tuesday to Friday the director will rehearse and record an average of fourteen scenes per day, working in the studio from 8 a.m. to 7 p.m. With such a tight shooting schedule, forty-five minutes is the maximum that can be allocated to each scene, which means that only two or three takes are normally recorded.

WEEK 3

This week is spent editing all the studio footage to produce four episodes of approximately twenty-six minutes each.

WEEK 4

This week is spent dubbing the episodes, which means inserting all necessary sound effects. As studio scenes are shot silently, apart from the dialogue, sound effects such as extras chatting in the pub, glasses clinking, and all the other sounds needed to create a convincing ambience, now have to be inserted. Background noise has to be carefully gauged, so that if the noise of traffic is audible in the background, its level will be heard to increase if someone opens a door to the outside.

WEEK 5

The final week in the cycle is spent doing exterior scenes. These will form part of the episodes being shot by the director who is simultaneously shooting interior scenes in the studio that week. The exteriors'

director will make a reconnaissance of locations on the Monday with the lighting cameraman, the sound engineer and the designer. Planning and shooting will then take place during the rest of the week, and the exterior scenes will be edited and dubbed on the following Saturday and Sunday.

And then, the five week cycle begins again...

The Billy Phen

The Billy Phenomenon

Of all the many characters to feature in Fair City,

none has ever had quite the impact on viewers that Billy Meehan had. Although he appeared in the series for less than a year, and has been gone since November 2001, the impression that the character made was enormous, and people still talk about him.

The most frequently heard refrain is "why did you have to kill Billy?" To which the answer is simple: he was too evil to remain in a soap long-term. Chancers, messers and run of the mill bad-boys can be accommodated, and even someone with a nasty side can be softened over time, or at least be seen to have redeeming features. Billy, however, could never have been turned into a lovable rogue. (This, after all, was a man who beat his pregnant wife so badly that she lost their baby). The sheer venom and the sense of menace that made him so repellent, yet so fascinating, meant that his days in Carrigstown were always numbered.

Quite a few people complained that the character was too gripping to kill off, and that he should have been sent to jail, thus facilitating a return to the series in the future. This was decided against on the grounds that it would inevitably be repetitious, bearing in mind the kind of stories that could involve Billy, and it was felt that it would be better to leave audiences wanting a little more and to go out on a high note.

Brilliantly played by Stuart Dunne, Billy entered the public consciousness in a way that few fictional characters do, and when he finally got his come-uppance on November 14th 2001, RTÉ recorded its highest viewership figures of that year.

Design

Mary Morrow is the senior designer for Fair City. Having formerly worked on *Glenroe, The Late Late Show, The Nine O'Clock News* and various sports programmes, she is an experienced designer and has responsibility for all sets and props seen on screen.

Mary's role is wide-ranging, involving everything from major undertakings such as redesigning McCoy's pub, to the small touches that add realism, such as organising framed photographs of cast members for the mantel-pieces of their "homes".

At any given time there will be at least four designers working on Fair City and this can increase to as many as six when the show's storyline calls for an elaborate set, like the intensive care unit for the Baby Jessica story, or a full courtroom, as was required for Leo's trial.

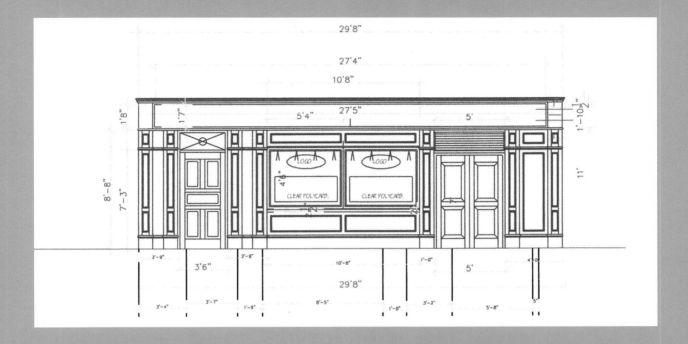

When a new set is needed meticulous research will be carried out to make sure that no mistakes are made in its design. For instance when an intensive care unit set was being planned, the design team visited the ICU in Crumlin Children's Hospital and took photographs of the unit, the equipment and all the ancillary items that are present in a real hospital setting. Likewise when considering what sort of look to give the new McCoys pub, the designer examined and photographed numerous pub frontages around the city before coming up with her design.

Design

Once designed, major sets will be constructed from architects' plans by one of a number of building firms associated with the show. These sets will usually be built on wheeled units with hand grips, which allows for good manoeuvrability, and sets will be constructed with ease of assembly and dismantling in mind.

Meanwhile buyers will visit shops and markets to source the props with which to dress the set, ensuring that the set in question acquires a realistic, lived–in look. Much attention is given to matching the style of a room with the personalities of the characters that will occupy it, and the designer will study character breakdowns and family profiles in order to tailor the design appropriately.

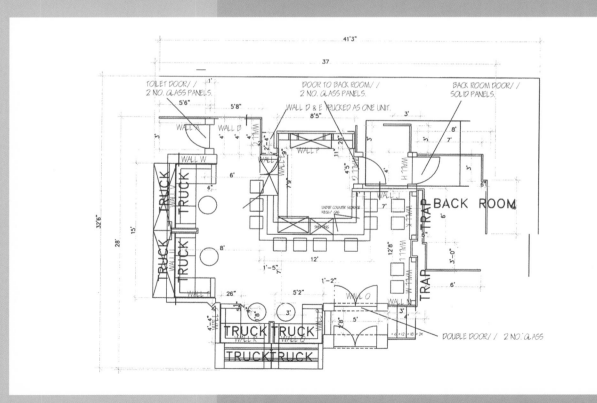

And do the cooker and washing machine in that spanking new kitchen actually work? No, is the answer most of the time; wiring and plumbing would add an unnecessary complication to the already demanding task of rigging and de-rigging. If a plot calls for it, however, the staging team can arrange for taps that produce water, fires that heat or ovens that cook – it's all part of the day's work for the design team on Fair City.

Eunice

FROM AROMATHERAPY, TO CAMPING IN THE PARK, NOTHING IS TOO OFF-THE-WALL FOR EUNICE

Costumes

Costumes

Clare Beegan is costume designer for Fair City. After training for three years in college, Clare worked freelance in the film industry before joining RTÉ, where she did costumes on a variety of programmes before being appointed costume designer for Fair City.

Clare has to read the script of every episode weeks in advance of shooting, marking each script for costume requirements. As well as choosing what each character should wear, the designer must also decide on changes of costume within an episode, and the continuity issues that arise regarding costumes, when episodes are shot out of sequence.

This means that if all of the week's scenes in McCoy's pub are being shot on Tuesday, and Kay appears in the pub on Tuesday, Wednesday and Thursday, then she needs to have three different outfits ready in her dressing room on the morning of shooting.

The designer must also factor in the mood of a character when choosing a costume for a given scene. So if, having read the script, the designer sees that a character is feeling downbeat, she might dress the character in a tracksuit. Or alternatively if the person is in good form and going out for a meal, or going on a date, then this will be reflected in a much more stylish costume.

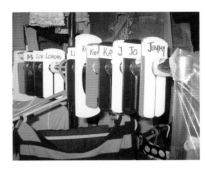

Clare also has to be aware of colour, so that a situation doesn't arise where, for example, the costumes are otherwise fine, but all of the men are wearing blue shirts.

Before the show was broadcast four nights a week, all the year round, the wardrobe department had the time to make garments, especially for big occasions like weddings. Due to time pressure this is no longer possible, and all outfits are now either borrowed from retailers or purchased.

A good deal of a costume designer's time is spent shopping for clothes. This is done without the actors being present, but as the designer knows the appropriate measurements - and has a clear vision of what's appropriate for the characters involved - there are usually few problems. Normally Clare can anticipate what individual actors will like or dislike, and while actors may be accommodated if they really dislike particular garments, generally the guiding rule is that the costume isn't a reflection of the actor's taste, but is chosen to be in keeping with the character.

Occasionally an actor will resist being made to look unattractive, but generally the cast recognise that the story dictates how the character ought to look. The guiding principle of being true to the character also applies to how long a costume should feature. People like Christy and Charlie keep costumes for quite a long time, as would be likely to happen in real life, whereas characters like Paul and Nicola acquire new outfits more frequently.

Making sure that costumes are washed, pressed, dry-cleaned and delivered to the correct dressing rooms each day is a major undertaking, and normally four wardrobe staff will work on Fair City each week. In addition to making sure that all of the cast are wearing the correct costume for any given scene, wardrobe staff also take pictures of every actor before a scene is shot. This is essential for continuity reasons, so that if an actor has his coat collar turned up while walking across the lot towards McCoys pub, that collar will also be turned up when the character enters the pub – even though the scenes may be shot days apart.

The wardrobe department keeps a large number of costumes in stock, with characters' outfits stored in alphabetical order. In addition to costumes for everyone currently in the series, wardrobe also have to hold onto the costumes of those who have left. This means that if a character has moved abroad but comes back for a funeral or some other story reason, costumes are readily available. Eventually, however, a

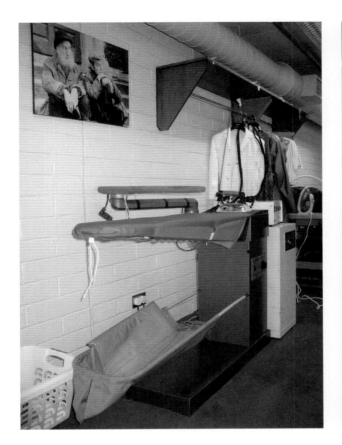
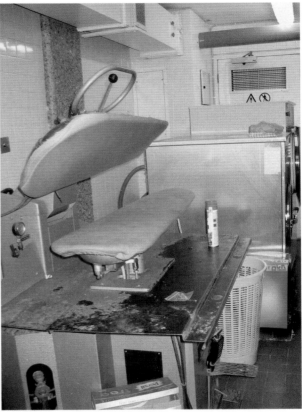

balance has to be struck between the economy of using existing costumes and the demands of storage space, and when outfits can no longer be retained they are usually sold off or given to charity shops.

So how many items of clothing does the Fair City wardrobe hold at any given time? Between seven and eight hundred, Clare Beegan reckons, and close to a thousand when footwear and items of jewellery are included. And they still have to find those sweaters for Christy – no wonder wardrobe is a busy department.

Weddings

Jimmy and Lorraine

Malachy and Kay

Paul and Nicola

Leo and Pauline

Weddings

Dermot and Jo

Jimmy and Robin

Ken and Geraldine

Eunice and Clive

Not Quite Wed

Marty and Tess renew their vows

dings ...

Lana almost marries Marcus

Make-up

Karen Nolan is in charge of make-up on Fair City. Having trained in RTÉ, Karen has worked on the show for the past four years.

No two days are ever the same in the make-up department, and the staff may be called upon to provide anything from everyday make-up to special effects that suggest illness or that show that someone has been beaten up.

Such special effects are not the norm, but they would still be required perhaps every two or three weeks. And if a character is badly bruised, then careful make-up work will be called for in subsequent episodes as the bruising is seen to fade over time.

Character Name: Jenny.

Base	Clinique Neutral 05.
Under Eye	YSL.
Powder	Clinique 08.
Blush	Angel.
Eyes	Pink freeze on lids + Electro on sockets. & under lashline.
Liner	Navy lines on top + Electro under eye
Mascara	Black
Brows	—
Lips	Cedar liner.

77	78	79	80.
Cedar + fuchsia fix.	Cedar + Kiehls	Cedar + Fushica	Cedar + fuschia.

Character Name: Jenny.

Hair Styles	
77	78
Blow dried straight. & down.	Ponytail — all back Mid-high pony — blue/navy rope scrunchie
79	80.
Down.	Hair down straight - parted centre - sides clipped back to centre with butterfly diamond clips

Make up

Ep/Sc		Script / Act
JENNY		
77/6	15·45·	HALPINS
77/10 ext	20·00	GALLEY
78/1	8·30	HALPINS LIVI
78/4 ext	12·20	GALLEY PUB
78/8	13·45	EFP SCHOOL Y.
78/12	15·50	HALPINS LIVI
79/1 ext	8·45	HALPINS LIVI
79/11	14·10	HALPINS LIVI
79/17	21·35	HALPINS KITC
80/8 ext	18·30	HALPINS KITC
80/16	20·40·	EFP LOT X PH
80/19	22·00	HALPINS LIVI

Sometimes a story will require a radical change in appearance, as happened in the Nicola cancer story, when the character began to lose her hair due to chemotherapy and a suitable wig had to be acquired by the make-up staff.

Five people from the make-up department are needed on the show every week, and the first make-up call each morning is at twenty past seven.

The members of the make-up team work closely with their wardrobe colleagues and much effort goes into making sure that continuity of appearance is maintained, a vital consideration

ion			Line Action
	D	I	*ROSS AND JENNY WORRY*
	N	I	*TRACEY OFFERS/BELA CONFID
	D	I	*ROSS ENCOURAGES JENNY TO
	D	I	*AIDAN SUGGESTS HE DO A B
	D	E	*JENNY ATTACKS A GIRL FOR
	D	I	*ROSS ENCOURAGES JENNY N
	D	I	*ROSS DECEIVES JENNY OVE
	D	I	*JENNY CHOOSES TO LIVE
G ROOM	N	I	*ROSS DISPLAYS A HINT O
	N	I	*ROSS LIES TO JENNY TO
	N	E	*JENNY ACTS COOL TOWAR
	N	I	*A DISILLUSIONED ROSS

Handwritten note:

Lang

Base - Nw 25
under eye - YSL
Powder - Clinque 08.
Blush - Harmony + Angel on cheeks.
eyes - Shroom... over + House
in sockets
liner - Black liquid on top + dark under
Mascara - Polock
Brows - Soft Smoke.
Lips - Maroon + Burnished Pink

Bobbi Brown Dusted over
face + neck

when so many scenes are shot

out of sequence.

As also happens with wardrobe, much use is made of digital cameras to record

each actor's hairstyle and make-up at the start of every scene. And if Jimmy's hair is wet from crossing the

rainy street to the Sandwich Bar on Wednesday, then make-up staff have to ensure that it's similarly wet

when he's filmed walking in for his sandwich – which may be shot the following Friday.

Hair-styling is an important element in the appearance of characters and every hair-band, clip or hair accessory of any kind is stored in duplicate by the make-up department. This means that if filming has taken place and then an accessory becomes broken or lost, continuity problems won't arise and shooting can continue with the appearance of the actor's hair being exactly as before.

So where is Carrigstown?

arrigstown

According to the Fair City 'bible' – a detailed document that records all information relating to the show – the imaginary district of Carrigstown is on Dublin's northside, bounded by Drumcondra to the north, the city centre to the south, East Wall to the east and Phibsboro to the west.

Kelly's

Carrigstown takes its name from the village that grew up around the quarries in which granite was mined until the early part of the twentieth century - *carraig* being the Irish word for rock.

O'Hanlon's

McCoy's, The Bookies and Doyles Shop

The 'bible' also informs us that in the 1920's there was a butchers, a greengrocers, a harness maker and a pub in place of the present premises.

Copeland House
Community Enterprise Centre

A bookies called Winner Alright closed down in 1989, and a Pizzeria called Pizza Action opened in its place.

This too closed in time, and the site is now occupied by the Bistro.

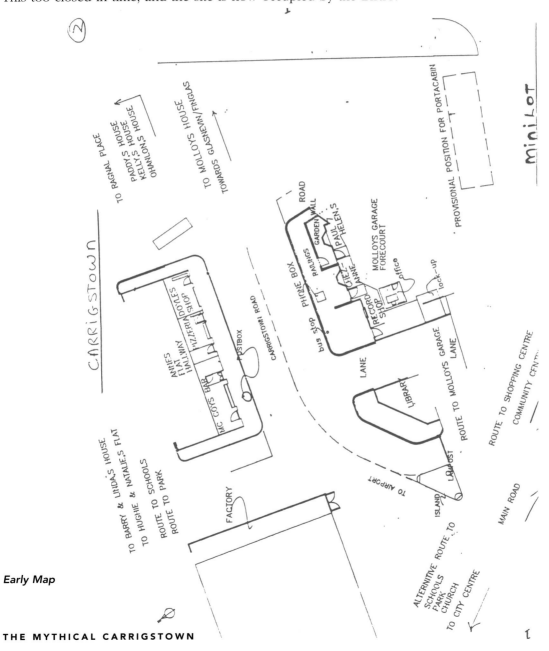

Early Map

Our final dip into the Fair City 'bible' tells us that the 1932 Housing Act reflected the then Government's desire to address the problem of tenement housing in the city centre. New housing schemes, including the one in Carrigstown, were planned by Dublin Corporation, and building work began in areas like Cabra in the nineteen thirties.

The Carrigstown housing scheme wasn't begun until 1946, however, following a temporary break in Corporation housing schemes as a result of a shortage of building materials during the war.

Casting

Casting is a critically important element in a successful series, and much thought goes into the casting of each new character. Consideration is given to physical appearance and accents, particularly when casting members of a family, or family members of an existing character. Decisions are usually taken after consultations between the executive producer, the series producer, and the series editor, with the executive producer having the final say.

The selection of particular actors may come about in number of ways. Perhaps an actor will have been seen giving a strong performance in a stage role. Or a CV on file may suggest a particular performer for a certain part. Often an actor will have screen-tested for another Fair City role and will have made an impression, despite not being cast in the role he or she sought. In these circumstances actors are frequently called back in when another part comes up.

And if those making the decisions didn't exercise good judgement, then Fair City would have a very different look . . .

Casting

For example, Stuart Dunne, who played psychopath Billy Meehan, originally auditioned for the part of Christy Phelan.

Aisling O'Neill
who plays Carol,
auditioned for the
part of Ava.

Una Kavanagh, who plays Heather, auditioned for the part of Geraldine.

David Johnston,
who plays Ken,
auditioned for the
part of Dr Jack.

Casting

Hilda Fay, who plays Tracey, auditioned for the part of Niamh.

Stella Fehilly, who plays Sorcha, auditioned for the part of Eleanor.

Casting

Casting, however, is not an exact science. Claudia Carroll, who plays Nicola Prendergast, was originally told that her character would appear for just one week – and twelve years later she's still playing the role!

Bela and Jimmy don't see eye to eye ...

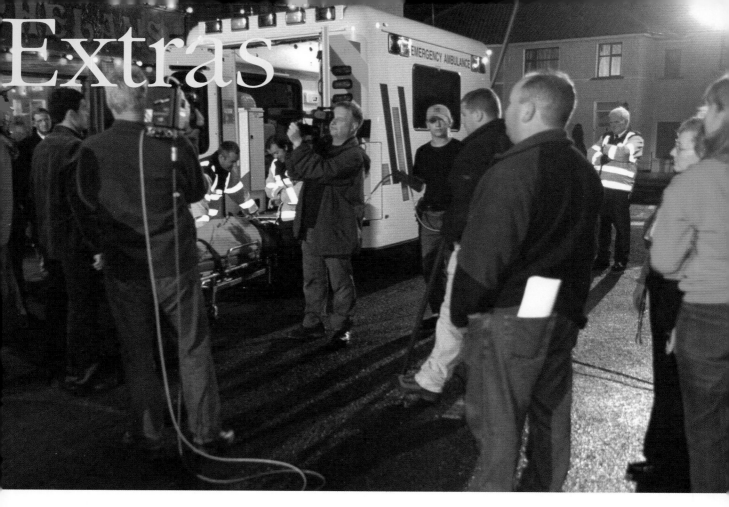

Extras

An extra on Fair City is defined as someone who appears on screen but says no lines.

Someone who says up to ten lines is classified as a Special Extra. Extras play an important part in creating a believable atmosphere, be it in the pub, at the shops or on the RTÉ lot where Fair City's specially built Carrigstown Road is located.

The show has been well served over the years by a long-standing team of dedicated extras who know the ropes and who can adapt with the flexibility called for when shooting four episodes every week. Many of the extras have come from the Equity extras' panel, others would be cast from those on file with the extras' casting director, and in an average week about one hundred and fifty extras are needed.

Each extra will bring three or four outfits along on the day of shooting, having first been briefed on the scene being filmed and on what constitutes appropriate clothing. Irrespective of the scene involved there are certain guidelines that always apply to extras' costumes – no large logos, no bright whites, no small checks, no thin stripes – the latter can cause a strobe effect when filmed!

Extras

Ideally, extras will be engaged about a week in advance, but with tight production schedules sometimes extras are hired the night before shooting. Days can be long, with extras often called in for an eight a.m. start, and while some scenes might be finished as early as three in

the afternoon, filming on the lot can occasionally go on till ten at night. Patience too is essential in a job that can entail a good deal of hanging around.

So why be an extra?

Barbara Bergin

Some people do it for the money, others regard it as a type of hobby – albeit one with payment, other do it out of a fascination with the programme itself. Students interested in the television industry will at times volunteer their services, as will aspiring actors.

For the most part acting roles are not cast from former extras. Occasionally, however, someone will make the transition from extra to established character, as happened when Barbara Bergin went from being an extra to playing the part of Natalie.

Sparring

Hannah

Pascal

Hannah & Pascal never did get it together,

Partners

```
>EUNICE
I just feel...we're really happy together the way we are and...well, I can't help
feeling, why rock the boat?

>CLIVE
I'm sorry if you feel that marrying me would be rocking the boat.

>EUNICE
Ah don't take it like that.  You know what I mean.

>CLIVE
No, actually, I'm not sure I do.

>EUNICE
I thought...I thought that maybe we could have the best of both worlds.

>CLIVE
I see.

>EUNICE
I mean, getting married at our age, Clive, it's a huge step.

>CLIVE
Getting married at any age is a huge step.

>EUNICE
Yes, but...

>CLIVE
It's only a problem if both parties don't want to take the step.  Which
clearly is the case here.

>
CLIVE RISES.  EUNICE RISES AFTER HIM.

>EUNICE
Please - don't leave like this.

>CLIVE
It's better I go.  I need...I need time to take this in. Goodnight.

>
CLIVE GOES.  EUNICE LOOKS AFTER HIM, CLEARLY UPSET.
```

Eunice & Clive, however, did - eventually

Life as a Fair City Actor

Una Crawford O'Brien is in her sixth season of playing Renee, a part she auditioned for when the Phelan family of Christy, Renee, Floyd and Farrah was brought into the series.

Although unlike the character she plays, Una is fond of Renee, admiring her gutsy qualities and the way the character has always striven to do her best for her family.

To prepare for her scenes, Una receives the week's scripts about three weeks in advance of shooting. If her character is part of an ongoing story however, then there won't be three weeks to study scenes and learn lines. Instead the actors will be rehearsing and recording, week after week, with very little time to learn lines in advance due to the pressures of shooting four episodes every week.

The schedule consists of rehearsals beginning on Saturday morning at nine and continuing until perhaps five o'clock. Una then uses Sunday to learn her lines in preparation for the producers' run that takes place on Monday morning. Monday afternoon is spent doing further work on lines, then shooting takes place on Tuesday, Wednesday, Thursday and Friday.

Fair City actors begin work at twenty past seven in the morning, at which time they report to Make-Up. Filming begins at twenty past

eight and continues all day with short breaks in the morning and afternoon and an hour-long break at lunchtime.

Studio scenes are recorded on Tuesday and Wednesday, scenes on RTÉ's outdoor lot are recorded on Thursday and location shooting normally takes place on Friday. Sometimes actors have to work very long days, as for instance when a night time scene has to be shot during summer. This can mean having to wait until quite late in the evening for darkness to fall, and shooting to begin.

Una recalls one memorable occasion when a difficult scene took until half two in the morning to shoot – with the next day's start still scheduled for twenty past seven!

So what is it like to be a Fair City actor and to be recognised constantly by the public? There is a certain pressure about having to look presentable, even during downtime, Una concedes, but she is philosophical, reasoning that having people appraising your appearance, and approaching you, simply comes with the job.

And do people differentiate between the actor and the character being played? Not always. Una tells the story of going into a shop to buy material for a quilt that she was making in her spare time. This was at the time that her fictional character of Renee had just taken over Carrigstown's corner shop, and the woman selling Una the quilt material expressed surprise that she would have the time for quilt-making – and she after opening a new shop!

Lighting Director

Each week on Fair City there will be one lighting director with responsibility for lighting all of the studio sets, and another lighting director who will look after lighting for the scenes shot on the lot or on location.

Lighting directors in RTÉ tend to come from a number of different backgrounds, some coming from the theatre, some having a technical background and others having a background in photography.

There are approximately twenty lighting directors in RTÉ and staff are seconded to Fair City on a rotational basis.

or

When filming is taking place in the studio the lighting crew consists of the lighting director, a lighting operator who will check on things like vision control and exposure levels, and an electrician.

For most studio scenes the lighting will be at a standard setting but for certain scenes a particular mood may be required, and lighting plays an important part in creating the right ambience. Thus if the director wants to shoot an intimate, romantic scene, this will be discussed in advance with the lighting director who can then light the scene softly and with warm hues.

Malachy's gaml

Malachy's gambling leads him astray

MALACHY'S GAMBLING LEADS HIM ASTRAY

The Theme Music

Fair City's theme music was composed by Adam Orpan Lynch and Hugh Drumm.

The brief given to the composers was to come up with a piece of music that would be easy on the ear, that would have a certain warmth, that would conjure up a feeling of Dublin and that would manage to reflect the general mood of the programme.

Hugh Drum and Adam Orpan Lynch

Music

It wasn't the easiest of tasks, given all the criteria that had to be met, and over twenty pieces were rejected as not being quite right before the present theme was produced. (Years later Adam Orpan Lynch would use some of these themes as incidental music when writing the score for the feature film *Night Train*.)

The present theme, with its catchy melody, felt right as soon as it was played, and since its introduction in 1995 it has become synonymous with Fair City.

Fair City Waltz *(Hugh Drumm/Adam Lynch)*

Sound

There are about thirty people employed in RTÉ's Sound Department and at any given time a sound supervisor and two sound operators will be working on Fair City.

The recording device most used on the programme is the boom microphone, which can rotate through 360 degrees and can also be tilted. If recording is taking place in a really tight corner, however – such as the back room in McCoy's pub – then a fishpole microphone will be used instead.

The sound crew will seek to get the microphone into the optimum position for recording so that each actor's dialogue is picked up at the right level, yet the sound supervisor must also take account of the camera angles, to ensure that the boom won't appear in shot. A further consideration for the sound crew is the lighting design for each scene and the need to ensure that the lights don't cast a shadow of the boom that can be picked up by the cameras.

Large sets like the old Blue Dolphin offices and Billy's apartment were challenging from a sound recording perspective, with wide open spaces in Blue Dolphin and a split level in Billy's apartment.

Another tricky area is the recording of crowded pub scenes where extras must mime in the background while the actors say their lines. If the extras whisper at all the sound can be picked up by sensitive boom mikes, and so it's important the miming be strictly adhered to with the background pub chatter dubbed in later.

And what else is dubbed in?
Everything from barking dogs to slamming doors, to rising and falling traffic noise. And on the dubbing database great attention is paid to detail - to the extent that a record is held of every householder's doorbell chime and every character's mobile ring tone, to ensure consistency.

Growing up in

Growing up in Fair City

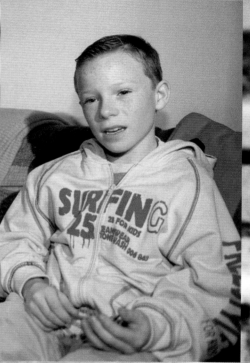

Oisin

Mondo

Fair City

TJ

Mark

Louise

Locations

Locations

The first location shooting for the series was done in Barron Place in Drumcondra. Later on, street scenes were shot in the Booterstown area, which was more convenient, being nearer to RTÉ.

Any shooting on location is likely to involve complications, however, such as be having to negotiate with residents, traffic noise, playing children or any of the other difficulties involved with shooting outside of a controlled environment.

For this reason it was decided to build a streetscape, known as the lot. In the early days the lot was in Ardmore Studios, near Bray, County Wicklow, then the present lot was built – and gradually extended over the years – in the grounds of RTÉ.

Locations

Notwithstanding the convenience and efficiency of shooting in a situation where everything can be controlled, it is still necessary to film quite a number of scenes on location.

In advance of shooting the director will do a reconnaissance with staff from Design, Lighting and Sound, then on the day of shooting the crew will attempt to film the sequence in the minimum number of takes.

Unlike on a feature film, where there would be a large crew and a number of assistant directors to liaise with local people and to create as controlled an environment as possible, shooting for Fair City is a much tighter operation, typically consisting of the actors in the scene plus a crew of perhaps eight or nine people.

In spite of the challenges, however, location shots enhance the sense of Fair City being an authentic representation of contemporary Dublin, and for this reason location filming features regularly in the show.

Editing

After shooting on an episode has finished, an editor will go through the episode scene by scene with the director. They will decide what constitutes the best take in each case and will choose which shots to retain and which to cut.

The executive producer and the series editor will then be sent this first cut, and they will examine each episode for running time. Three of the weekly Fair City episodes have a running time of twenty-four minutes and thirty seconds, while the Wednesday night broadcast is a minute longer at twenty-five minutes and thirty seconds.

The executive producer and the series editor will go through the written script, marking where cuts can be made so that the episode ends up with the correct running time.

Most episodes are a minute or two over schedule at the first-cut stage, and in addition to getting the timing right, the series editor and executive producer will now seek, by virtue of judicious pruning, to improve the flow of the episode, making it pacier and more dynamic.

The episode will then go back to the editing suite and a final edit will be done to produce the finished product that viewers will see on screen.

Original Cast

Original Cast Members

Of the cast that began working on Fair City back in 1989, five actors are still with the show:

Members

Sarah McDowall plays the part of Suzanne.

Sarah was only seven when the show began. At the time her aunt was an actress, and she mentioned to Sarah and her sister Alex that RTÉ was looking for youngsters for its new urban drama series.

Both the McDowall sisters were cast as members of the fictional Doyle family. Whereas Alex left after a few years, Sarah stayed with the show, growing up before the viewers' eyes as her character made the transition from innocent child to confident young woman.

Sarah concedes that juggling school attendance and homework with the shooting of episodes required a certain amount of flexibility, but RTÉ often facilitated her by shooting her scenes late in the afternoon, when she was finished school. Later on, when Sarah was doing her Leaving Certificate, it was agreed that she would film only during the holiday period.

By now so much of Sarah's life has been spent playing Suzanne that the role is second nature to her, and she takes it in her stride when members of the public address her as Suzanne - and ask after Rita and Bela!

Favourite storylines of Sarah's include the first-love story with Damien, the unfolding of Suzanne's turbulent relationship with Floyd and the story where her screen father, Bela, had to cope with cancer.

Original Cast

Pat Nolan plays the part of Barry.

Pat Nolan competed successfully for the part of Barry in auditions held when the first series of Fair City was being cast.

Having left school at fifteen, Pat worked as a postman by day and did amateur drama at night. He moved on to semi-professional acting and quit the day job when offered a role in a production of *The Mousetrap* that toured Switzerland.

Unlike Barry, Pat is married with two children, and it was while acting in Switzerland that he met his wife, Rebecca Roper, with whom he later founded *Black Box Theatre Company*. Despite the fact that the character of Barry has carried some major storylines over the years, Pat has always managed to find time for stage work, both with Black Box and as a freelance actor.

Even the most carefully orchestrated time management can go awry occasionally, however, and Pat can still recall the scheduling nightmare that arose when the wedding of Paul and Helen was being shot. Firstly an actor took ill and scripts had to be frantically re-written, and then, having shot the scenes, the recordings were stolen from the cameraman's car and the scenes had to be re-shot!

Pat's favourite storylines include the Baby Alice drama, the schoolgirl Niamh's false accusations story and the Sorcha/Barry/Ross triangle.

In May 2005 Pat won the Rose d'Or at the Lucerne Festival for best male performer in a television soap.

Members

Tony Tormey plays the part of Paul.

Tony Tormey worked as a laboratory technician in St James Hospital before becoming an actor. He graduated from the Gaiety School of acting, then went straight into Joe Dowling's acclaimed production of *Borstal Boy.*

On being sent by his agent to read for a part in Fair City, Tony was taken aback to find that hundreds of other hopefuls were in RTÉ, all auditioning for parts in the new show. Notwithstanding the numerical odds, he read for the parts of Barry and Paul. He was delighted to be cast as Paul, and sixteen years later still enjoys the role.

And does he like the character, as a person? "I love him – but I wouldn't want to be him," says Tony. He admits that in playing Paul he draws on some elements of his own personality, but points out that Paul can be naive and impulsive, thus landing himself in all sorts of scrapes. Having said that, Tony really likes the fact that whatever his other flaws, Paul has always been a devoted father.

Playing a high profile part for such a long time means that Tony has become accustomed to all sort of public reactions – from friendly praise to people sitting themselves down at his table in restaurants to give him an earful, to people who don't differentiate between fiction and reality and who lecture him on Paul's behaviour. And once, memorably, there was the viewer who asked, in all seriousness, if when she and her husband were looking at Paul on the television, could he in turn look into the camera and see them?!

The most memorable storylines to date for Tony were the death of his partner, Helen, with all the attendant emotional trauma, and the Barry/Niamh/Paul triangle with its powerful ingredient of friendship betrayed.

Jean Costello plays the part of Rita.

Jean Costello was touring the UK with her one-woman show *Shades of the Jelly Woman* when the call came from RTÉ to audition for its new urban drama.

Margaret Gleeson, Fair City's first Executive Director, had seen Jean in her one-woman show and asked her to read for the part of Rita Doyle. Jean landed the part and has been playing the indefatigable Rita ever since.

Although she says that it took her a while to get into the character of Rita, Jean loves playing her and describes her as a bit of a softie. Nevertheless Jean particularly enjoyed the storylines concerning her husband Bela's philandering and the break-up of their marriage – stories that ultimately showed Rita's inner strength.

And despite the fact that over a decade has passed since the fictitious couple split up, Jean is still asked the same question by fans of the show. . . "When are you getting back with Bela?"!

Members

Tom Jordan plays the part of Charlie.

Tom Jordan was already an established television actor before joining the cast of Fair City, having appeared in shows such as *Strumpet City*, *The Riordans* and *Inside*.

Tom was also a well-know stage actor, and had finished a two-year stint as Artistic Director of the Lyric Theatre in Belfast shortly before Fair City was first mooted. Having heard that auditions were being held for RTÉ's new urban drama, Tom read for the part of Charlie Kelly, and was pleased to land such a central role, with Darragh Kelly cast as his son and Ger Ryan as his daughter.

Asked how he feels about Charlie, Tom says that there are some elements of Charlie that are drawn from his own personality – but quickly points out that his wife and grown-up daughter have ensured that he would never be as politically incorrect as Charlie in dealing with the opposite sex!

Although Charlie is often a little old-fashioned, Tom nonetheless admires the character for his basic decency and unquestionable integrity. And after sixteen years he still really enjoys playing a man who, although somewhat conformist, is also well-read and intelligent.

Memorable storylines for Tom over the years include the murder of his son, Tony, the light-hearted story regarding the hot-dog stand, and the trauma that Charlie faced after accidentally killing Johnno.

Scheduling

Scheduling

The formula for an average week is as follows:

54 scenes in studio.

12 scenes on the lot, the streetscape located in the grounds of RTÉ.

Between 7 and 9 scenes on location.

With Fair City running four nights a week, fifty-two weeks a year, scheduling is critically important. Months in advance of shooting a given week's episodes, it will be decided how many scenes can be filmed, and the proportion of indoor, outdoor and location scenes.

An assistant producer in the Script Department decides on story requirements and, having juggled with the numbers, informs the locations' producer several months in advance of location requirements.

Mary Martin

This long lead-in is essential as permission may have to be sought for filming, and specialists may need to be engaged – for example when McCoy's pub was being burned down stuntmen had to be booked in advance, to ensure their availability on the night of shooting.

The Script Department co-ordinates with the designer, who will need notice both for costume purposes and for sourcing or manufacturing props or other set requirements. The final scheduling task is done when a director's week of filming approaches. At that stage schedulers will map out each day for the director, calculating how many scenes can be shot, and what constitutes the most efficient shooting order.

The Opening Sequence

There have been three opening sequences in Fair City. The original was shot in 1989. The second was shot in the mid-nineties when John Lynch, the then Executive Producer, decided that the opening sequence needed modernising. Much planning went into devising a series of images that would conjure up a warm, atmospheric image of Dublin.

John Hayes designed the sequence in conjunction with John Lynch, and only when everything had been laid out in advance on storyboards did shooting go ahead.

Sequence

Filming was done over four days, and instead of the usual use of video, the sequence was shot on film to get the stylish, glossy look of the finished piece.

Shooting was done both early in the morning and late in the evening to create the right kind of mood and to capture a certain sort of light. (And in a Hitchcockian touch, the man seen walking on Sandymount strand with the little girl was actually the designer of the sequence, with his young daughter.)

The final shot looking up along the Liffey was filmed from the roof of O'Connell Bridge House and took hours to get right. Even then there were problems with cloudy skies, and the effect of the sunlight sparkling on the water had to be painstakingly inserted in the studio, frame by frame, to enhance the final shot.

The finished product justified all the effort however, and for ten years the opening sequence remained unchanged - apart from the digital insertion of the Millennium Bridge.

In order to be compatible with wide-screen format, a new opening sequence, designed by and directed by Michael Mc Keon, was recorded in 2005. Shot on film and designed to show the changing face of Dublin, it was first broadcast in September 2005.

Leo's protestations that

he's not a murderer

don't keep him out of Court . . .

Broadcasting

Broadcasting Frequency

Back in 1989, who would have thought that the show would increase in output by almost 700%?

Yet such has been its popularity that Fair City has gone from 30 episodes in its first season to its current output of 208 episodes per year. The season has traditionally begun each Autumn, usually in the first week of September.

1989/1990	Once a week	No summer broadcasts
1990/1991	Twice a week	No summer broadcasts
1991/1992	Twice a week	No summer broadcasts
1992/1993	Twice week	No summer broadcasts
1993/1994	Twice a week	No summer broadcasts
1994/1995	Twice a week	No summer broadcasts
1995/1996	Twice a week	No summer broadcasts

Frequency

1996/1997	Twice a week	Once a week in summer
1997/1998	Twice a week	Once a week in summer
1998/1999	Twice a week	Once a week in summer
1999/2000	Three times a week	Once a week in summer
2000/2001	Three times a week	Twice a week in summer
2001/2002	Four times a week	Twice a week in summer
2002/2003 Onwards	Four times a week all year round	

1000th Episode

In December 2001, a milestone was reached and the cast celebrated filming the 1000th episode of Fair City.

Floor Manager

The job of the floor manager is to co-ordinate everything that happens on the studio floor. The crew for an episode of Fair City can be anything from ten to fifteen people, with representatives from lighting, sound, costume and make-up in attendance.

While the director runs the show from the control box, the floor manager is in the centre of things and acts as the director's eyes and ears on the studio floor. With new actors and extras sometimes feeling nervous, an important part of the floor manager's job is to put people at ease and to create a good working environment.

RTÉ floor managers are trained in-house, with many of them having some kind of a stage background. Once trained, each floor manager will be allocated to a range of programmes within the station.

When a floor manager is seconded to Fair City he or she will receive scripts of the episodes to be shot, three or four weeks in advance. Having read the scripts, and studied camera angles and cues for entrances and exits, the floor manager will attend the Saturday rehearsal and make detailed notes of each actor's movements.

Shooting begins on Tuesday, and at the start of each scene the floor manager will ensure that the cameras are in the right position, that the actors are standing by and know their moves and that all of the crew are ready to do their jobs when the director calls for action.

And the most important attributes for a good floor manager? According to one veteran, diplomacy and the ability to anticipate problems – and prevent them from arising – are the true hallmarks of a good floor manager.

Parents And Children

RTÉ Guide

PROGRAMMES: JUNE 5 - 11, 2004
PRICE: €1.50, N IRELAND £1.00

PUT TOGETHER
THE PERFECT BEAUTY TRAVEL BAG

IRELAND'S
BEST-SELLING MAGAZINE

www.rteguide.ie

RTÉ GUIDE

GREAT VALUE
AT JUST
€1.50

WEDDING JITTERS IN EASTENDERS
Sonia and Martin elope!

ROBBIE KEANE EXCLUSIVE
"It's great to have Roy back"

MARIAN KEYES EXCLUSIVE
Reveals her side of the story

CRAIG DOYLE
Returns to RTÉ with a new style chat show

FAIR CITY REVELATIONS
END OF THE AFFAIR
Can they bear to end their classroom romance?

RTÉ ONE / RTÉ NET2 / TG4 / TV3 / BBC / UTV / C4 / SATELLITE / CABLE / RADIO

Fair City characters have featured on the front cover of the RTÉ Guide on many occasions. Remember these?

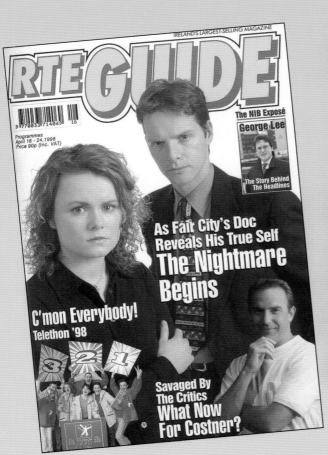

RTÉ Guide

Cover 1:

MARIO ROSENSTOCK | NASTY NICK | DONAL McCANN

RTÉ **GUIDE**

IRELAND'S LARGEST-SELLING MAGAZINE

Programmes: December 9 – 15, 2000 Price: £1 (Inc. VAT) €1.27

Dangerous Liaisons

Tensio... high...

At Home with CATHY

HER MOST CANDID INTERVIE...

"Sometimes I get upset when I'm...

Cover 2:

INTERVIEWS | DAMON ALBARN | DEREK MOONEY | NAOMI LYNCH

RTÉ **GUIDE**

IRELAND'S LARGEST-SELLING MAGAZINE

Programmes: Jan 22 – 28, 2000

Price: £1

(Inc. VAT) €1.27

Marian Finucane

BUILDING ON THE PAST

Posh Spice Reveals All

...t have Harry, ...er will Dolores

Cover 3:

...SIDE | JOE DUFFY AND HIS MA | KEITH WOOD – HOOKED ON LOVE

RTÉ **GUIDE**

...LAND'S LARGEST-...ING MAGAZINE

Programmes: ...1 – 7, 2000

...£1 (Inc. VAT)

...ALL

Wedded ...liss...

...hen Shelley ...rrives

...ND IN GLENROE . . .

Will Dick Moran turn up?

MILLIONAIRE SPECIAL | DESTINY'S CHILD | JOHN OX

40 YEARS 1961 2001

RTE **GUIDE**

IRELAND'S LARGEST-SELLING MAGAZINE

Programmes:
nuary 6 - 12, 2001
ce: £1 (Inc. VAT) €1.27

The Andy
Williams
Interview

A Love Divided
Kay and Malachy face the most challenging decision of their lives

Weight Watchers

FREE INSIDE!
32-page
WEIGHT WATCHERS magazine

9 770033 714069 01

NICOLAS CAGE | DESMOND GUINNESS | SARAH LANCASHIRE AND KIAN'S DIARY

RTE **GUIDE**

IRELAND'S
LARGEST-SELLING
MAGAZINE

Programmes:
August 5 - 11, 2000
Price: £1 (Inc. VAT)
€1.27

WIFE EILY AND MOTHER MAY
Remembering
Frank Patterson

STREET ROMANCE
Rita Finds Love

RIVERDANCE
At Home With
Bill Whelan

FAIR CITY'S
CLAUDIA CARROLL

'I'd hate to be like Nicola'

9 770033 714069 31

Stage Manager

The stage manager's job is to ensure that all of the cast and extras are on the right set at the right time so that precious studio time is not lost.

Stage managers generally come from a theatrical background, although the role of a stage manager in television differs considerably from its theatrical equivalent.

Because television is a more complex undertaking than stage drama the floor manager – who has overall control - is responsible for many of the duties that a stage manager would undertake in theatre. This frees the stage manager to concentrate on co-ordinating all activities relating to the cast.

The stage manager will call each of the actors, ensuring that everyone is present for the Saturday rehearsal. The stage manager will also make sure that each actor arrives on set punctually, having first attended make-up and wardrobe calls.

As a back-up to the floor manager's records, the stage manager will also record the blocking out of the actors' moves, as agreed at the Saturday rehearsal. In general the stage manager will work in tandem with the floor manager to ensure that the correct cast members are in the right location when the director is ready to start a scene.

Working so closely with the actors means that the ability to get on with people is an essential attribute for the job. Fair City has a reputation as a happy show to work on and part of the reason for this is undoubtedly because of the skills of its experienced stage managers.

It had to end in tears when Floyd fell for Heather -

without knowing that she was his half-sister ...

Specials

Over the years Fair City has had a number of one-hour specials. The broadcasting of these programmes tended to be on occasions like Christmas Day, the first night of the Autumn schedule or where a particularly high point had been reached in a storyline.

In 2002, when the programme began being broadcast four nights a week, all the year round, a different type of opportunity for specials arose. In order to allow cast and crew to take holidays it was decided to film week-long specials simultaneously with normal shooting. In this way production could shut down for holidays without a gap appearing in the schedules.

From a story-telling point of view these specials provided an opportunity to tackle in some depth issues of importance to contemporary Irish society. Hilary Reynolds, who has written a number of specials, has developed a lot of expertise in this area. Originally an actor on the show – for several years she played *femme fatale* Shelley – Hilary made the move to

Hilary Reynolds

Specials

the other side of the cameras and
began writing scripts for the show.
In 2002 Hilary was asked to do a
story against the backdrop of the
educational system. She collaborated
with series editor Kevin McHugh,
and between them they developed a

gripping story that dealt with date rape and teen suicide.

There was a very positive public reaction to these episodes, and the

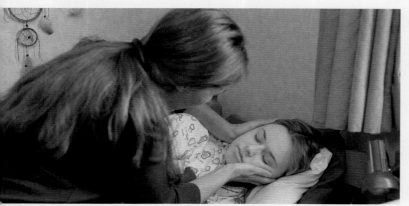

following year another week-
long special was broadcast.
This dealt with the moral
dilemma of a Catholic priest
who felt that he hadn't done

enough to prevent the sexual abuse of children. With a strong performance by T.P. McKenna as the priest, and with story again by Kevin McHugh and Hilary Reynolds, this made for compelling drama.

One of the problems in creating specials has been the fact that most of their characters were not Fair City regulars – many of whom were tied-up with the simultaneous shooting of normal episodes. This meant that the

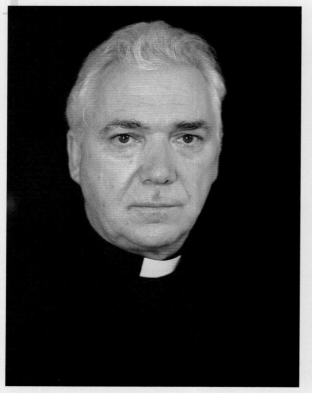

viewers had little time to get to know and care for the new characters.

This difficulty was addressed in the special that was broadcast at the end

of 2004, both by telling the story over two weeks instead of one, and by

using many of the characters from the previous church-related special.

With a cast that included such established actors as Anna Manahan, Bosco Hogan, T P McKenna and Frank Grimes, this special, which dealt with church politics, the legal system - and most poignantly - the human cost to a family that suffered child abuse, caused a considerable stir.

Knowing that the area of abuse was a highly sensitive and contentious one, writer Hilary Reynolds did a great deal of research, worked closely with the support group One in Four, and went through numerous drafts with series editor Kevin McHugh before the highly-charged episodes were shot.

The most recent special was broadcast for two weeks in the summer of 2005, and featured the moral dilemmas faced by Mondo as he found himself getting out of his depth while pursuing his dreams of material success. Set against a backdrop of property speculation and insider trading, and with story by Hilary Reynolds and Kevin McHugh, it looked at the murkier side of yuppie life and presented the popular character of Mondo, played by George McMahon, with some life and death decisions.

Series Publicist

Tara O'Brien handles all the press and media work relating to the show.

On average two to three articles per week concerning Fair City appear in the national press. Tara attends the producer's run each Monday morning, after which she decides which scenes to have photographed for publicity and archive purposes.

In dealing with press stories the publicist has to strike a balance between not revealing too much too soon about unfolding plotlines, and generating interest in the series by whetting the appetite of readers - and potentially viewers – concerning exciting story developments.

'Fair City' producers reject priest's criticism of storyline

ALISON HEALY
AND ANNE LUCEY

The producers of the *Fair City* TV soap have rejected criticism from the pulpit about a storyline involving clerical sex abuse.

The storyline revolves around an ex-priest, played by T.P. McKenna, who breaks the seal of Confession in the hope of bringing an abuser to justice.

Father Kevin McNamara, a priest in Killarney, told parishioners at the weekend that he had been "stung" and hurt when he read that the storyline involved a priest breaking the seal of Confession.

He told Mass-goers at St Mary's Cathedral on Saturday evening that ~~the seal of Confession is never broken~~

She said the writers wanted t show the motivation behind the priest's decision to break the se confession. The character, Fath Tom Mitchell, felt it was more important to help an abuse vict get justice, than to keep the sea Confession.

"He didn't do it easily. He weighed it up very carefully a decided that supporting a vict abuse was better than keeping vow," the spokeswoman said.

"I can't see how that would people from going to Confess The Confession part of the st was just a sideline compared the abuse issue."

She said the *Fair City* write handled the issue very sensit and had put a lot of effort int researching the issue with th

Father Kevin McNamara: "seal of ~~Confession is never broken~~

When controversies occur, as happened with the story of Kay's abortion, and more recently with the story of child abuse and the response of the Catholic Church, the publicist has an important role to play. In conjunction with the series producer, the publicist is responsible for responding to how the media portray Fair City's handling of delicate issues and for ensuring that it's made clear that the script team strives to be fair and balanced when tackling controversial topics.

Tara contends that the Irish media are usually quite reasonable in not prying into cast members' private lives. Having said that, actors in the show are frequently in demand for interviews and vox pops - part of the price for starring in a high-profile series - and the channelling of these requests is also part of the publicist's job.

EVENING HERALD TUESDAY 17 AUGUST 2004 **21**

NEWS

SOAP SHOCKER: Sorcha's entanglement with student comes to light

Teacher's affair to rock Fair City

Controversy ov Fair City storyli

Priests found the storyline in "Fair City" dealing with the breaking of the seal of confession, "distressing and hurtful".

Fr Kevin McNamara of Killarney speaking to The Irish Catholic this week said: "The seal of confession is sacrosanct. It is absolute. It is a no-go area.

ANNE RYAN

their feelings too", Fr McNamara said that it is very offensive to suggest a confessor can break the seal of confession.

Fr McNamara said this treatment of the sacrament showed a lack of understanding of the whole "faith dimen-

fessed to him s
he couldn't ev
habit, and hid
prevent himsel

He said a p
sion would be
someone who
ual offence ne
and to go for
penitent wo
warned to leav

Opening of the

In March 2005, Marty Whelan

new McCoy's

opened the new McCoy's

Funerals

Ashes to ashes,

The Fair City Quiz

How much of a Fair City aficionado are you?
Put your knowledge to the test:

1. How did Jimmy's first wife, Lorraine, die?

2. What was Jo working as when Dermot first met her?

3. How many times has Leo been married?

4. Who is the odd-man-out in never having served a sentence in prison – Lorcan, Leo, Harry, Barry or Floyd?

5. Which character is Eunice's nephew?

6. Of what crime were Richard and Yvonne guilty when they left Carrigstown and fled the country?

7. What is Myles Byrne's rank as a Garda?

8. Apart from the fact that she really loved Leo, why else did Lana have reservations about marrying Marcus?

9. In what foreign country did Paschal serve with the Irish army?

10. As Barry and Linda tried to cope with the death of baby Alice, it emerged that Barry wasn't the biological father. Who was?

11. Who was kidnapped by a man who subsequently became a colleague?

12. For what British soccer team did Jimmy Doyle get a trial in his youth?

13. Dermot once dated Annette, but he ended the relationship when he discovered – what?

ANSWERS

1. She was killed in a hurricane. **2.** A librarian. **3.** Four marriages – Petula, Sandi, Pauline and Lana. **4.** Barry. **5.** Malachy. **6.** They were guilty of a hit-and-run motor accident. **7.** Detective Sergeant. **8.** He was gay. **9.** The Congo. **10.** Bela. **11.** Niamh. **12.** Manchester United. **13.** Annette is an alcoholic. **14.** Hairdressers. **15.** Balbriggan. **16.** Helen Doyle. She left Mike to run away with Paul. **17.** The nanny had run off with Oisin. **18.** A window cleaner. **19.** Shelly, who had had an affair with Harry, the father of the bride. **20.** Mondo repaired his car in the garage. **21.** Hughie. **22.** To protect animals in the rain forest. **23.** True. **24.** His father killed his mother, then committed suicide. **25.** Two children, Oisin and Rachel

14. What did Dolores and Shelley work at when they were single?

15. Where did Ray, Angela and Mondo live originally?

16. Who left her prospective husband at the altar to run away with another man?

17. Why did Nicola once drop everything to travel urgently to Wales with Paul?

18. What was Christy's occupation when the Phelans first arrived in Carrigstown?

19. Who caused a scene at the wedding of Jimmy and Lorraine?

20. How did Seamus McAleer and Mondo meet for the first time?

21. Eunice has a younger son than Christy who works on a cruise ship. Who is he?

22. Suzanne left college for what idealistic purpose?

23. In his younger days Barry studied for the priesthood. True or false?

24. How did Damien end up caring for his brother and sister?

25. How many children does Paul have?

Actors featuring in the book include:

Jean Costello	AS	Rita Doyle	
Jim Bartley	AS	Bela Doyle	
Sarah McDowall	AS	Suzanne Doyle	
David Mitchell	AS	Jimmy Doyle	
Aoife Doyle	AS	Louise Doyle	
Kira Carroll	AS	Helen Doyle	
Ciara O'Callaghan	AS	Yvonne Doyle	
Orlaith Wrafter	AS	Robin Doyle	
Pat Nolan	AS	Barry O'Hanlon	
Doreen Keogh	AS	Mary O'Hanlon	
Caroline Rothwell	AS	Linda O'Hanlon	
Tony Tormey	AS	Paul Brennan	
Deanna Kissane	AS	Rachel Brennan	
Simon O'Driscoll	AS	Oisin Brennan	
Jim Reid	AS	Jack Flynn	
Aine Ni Mhuiri	AS	Lili Corcoran	

Charlie Roberts	AS	Paddy Clarke
Martina Flynn	AS	Anne Clarke
Eanna MacLiam	AS	Johnny One
Pat Leavy	AS	Hannah Finnegan
Martina Stanley	AS	Dolores Molloy
Paul Raynor	AS	Harry Molloy
Maeve McGrath	AS	Lorraine Molloy
Stephen Swift	AS	Wayne Molloy
Eddie Naessens	AS	Jack Shanahan
Garret Keogh	AS	Eamon Clancey
Seamus Moran	AS	Mike Gleeson
Joan O'Hara	AS	Eunice Phelan
Tom Hopkins	AS	Christy Phelan
Una Crawford-O'Brien	AS	Renee Phelan
Simon Keogh	AS	Floyd Phelan
Joe Hanley	AS	Hughie Phelan

Barbara Bergin	AS	Natalie Carr	Mick Nolan	AS	Ray O'Connell
Joan Brosnan Walsh	AS	Mags Kelly	Anne Kent	AS	Angela O'Connell
Tom Jordan	AS	Charlie Kelly	Hilda Fay	AS	Tracey McGuigan
Sheila McWade	AS	Kay McCoy	Aaron Harris	AS	Miles Byrne
Shane McDaid	AS	Stephen McCoy	Stella Feehily	AS	Sorcha Byrne
Gerard Byrne	AS	Malachy Costello	Katie Cullen	AS	Jenny Byrne
Paul McGlinchey	AS	Danny McCusker	Tommy O'Neill	AS	John Deegan
Alan Smyth	AS	Eoghan Healy	Jamie Belton	AS	Ross O'Rourke
Lenny Hayden	AS	Lenny Wilson-Drake	Dave Duffy	AS	Leo Dowling
Claudia Carroll	AS	Nicola Prendergast	Tatianna Ouliankina	AS	Lana Dowling
Kate Binchy	AS	Anne Prendergast	Yuri Stepanov	AS	Sergei Borodin
Fiona Sinnott	AS	Philippa Prendergast	Lise-Ann McLaughlin	AS	Pauline Fitzpatrick
David Heap	AS	Donal Maher	Maclean Burke	AS	Damien Halpin
Alan Archbold	AS	Richard Ashton	Sabina Brennan	AS	Tess Halpin
Rebecca Smith	AS	Annette Daly	Paul Lee	AS	Marty Halpin
Clelia Murphy	AS	Niamh Cassidy	Ryan O'Shaughnessy	AS	Mark Halpin
Deirdre Lawless	AS	Gina Cassidy	Joe Cassidy	AS	Frank Monaghan
Carla Young	AS	Kira Cassidy	James Donnelly	AS	Derek Devlin
George McMahon	AS	Mondo O'Connell	Linda McDonnell	AS	Pat Morrissey

Aisling O'Neill	AS	Carol Foley		Hilary Reynolds	AS	Shelley O'Connor
Killian O'Sullivan	AS	Lorcan Foley		Frank Melia	AS	Sean McCann
Stuart Dunne	AS	Billy Meehan		Sorcha Furlong	AS	Orla Kirwan
Ciaran O'Brien	AS	Joey Meehan		Gemma Doorly	AS	Sarah O'Leary
Frank Smith	AS	Anthony Farrell		Vinnie McCabe	AS	Seamus McAleer
Fran Brennan	AS	Mick Mahoney		Rachel Kavanagh	AS	Lauren McAleer
James Rowe	AS	Clive Dunstan		Janet Phillips	AS	June Pearson
Seamus Power	AS	Dermot Fahey		T P McKenna	AS	Fr. Mitchell
Peg Power	AS	Mary Fahey		Anna Manahan	AS	Ursula Cruise
Rachel Sarah Murphy	AS	Jo Fahey		Frank Grimes	AS	Fr. Lawlor
David Johnston	AS	Ken Fahey		Bosco Hogan	AS	Bishop Dowling
Carmel Stephens	AS	Geraldine Fahey		Brian Doherty	AS	Ben Quirke
Anne-Marie Horan	AS	Eleanor Coughlan		Feidlim Cannon	AS	Aidan Quirke
David O'Brien	AS	Marcus Lamb		Tony Rohr	AS	Fr. Rowe
Una Kavanagh	AS	Heather Daly		Paddy Dawson	AS	Seamus Mannion
Tom O'Meara	AS	Brendan Daly		Barry Barnes	AS	Kieran Roddy
Lise Hearns	AS	Ava Spillane		Lynn Styles	AS	Emma Nicholson
Brendan Cauldwell	AS	Pascal Mulvey		Doireann Ni Chorragain	AS	Ali O'Shea
Ian Kenny	AS	TJ Deegan		Bryan Murray	AS	Bob Charles